DESTINATION:
EARTH

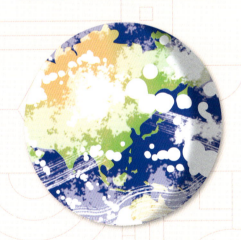

SALLY SPRAY AND
MARK RUFFLE

First published in Great Britain in 2023
by Wayland
© Hodder and Stoughton Limited, 2023

HB ISBN: 978 1 5263 2077 3
PB ISBN: 978 1 5263 2078 0

Editor: Paul Rockett
Design and illustration: Mark Ruffle
www.rufflebrothers.com

MIX
Paper from
responsible sources
FSC® C104740
FSC
www.fsc.org

Printed in Dubai

Wayland
An imprint of Hachette Children's Group
Part of Hodder & Stoughton
Carmelite House
50 Victoria Embankment
London EC4Y 0DZ

An Hachette UK company
www.hachette.co.uk
www.hachettechildrens.co.uk

Picture credits:
Page 30 NASA/Robert and Marit
Jentoft-Nilsen, based on MODIS data/
JPL; page 31 NASA/JSC

SAFETY PRECAUTIONS

We recommend adult supervision at all
times while doing the experiments in this
book. Always be aware that ingredients
may contain allergens, so check the
packaging for allergens if there is a risk of
an allergic reaction. Anyone with a known
allergy must avoid these.

- Wear an apron and cover surfaces.
- Tie back long hair.
- Ask an adult for help with cutting.
- Check all ingredients for allergens.
- Clear up all spills straight away.

Contents

Meet the team

Dr Bott

Mo

Stella

Max

Xing

Melody

Welcome to Space Station Academy, the amazing interstellar school that travels through space. Come on board and learn about our solar system.

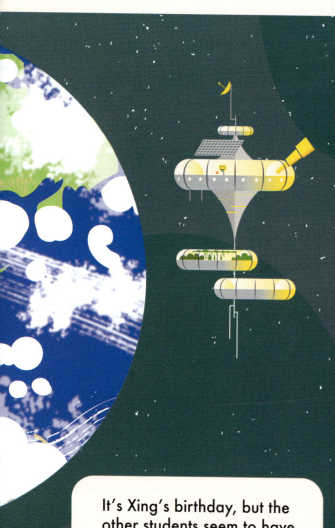

It's Xing's birthday, but the other students seem to have forgotten. They are busy getting ready to visit their home planet, Earth.

I'm here!

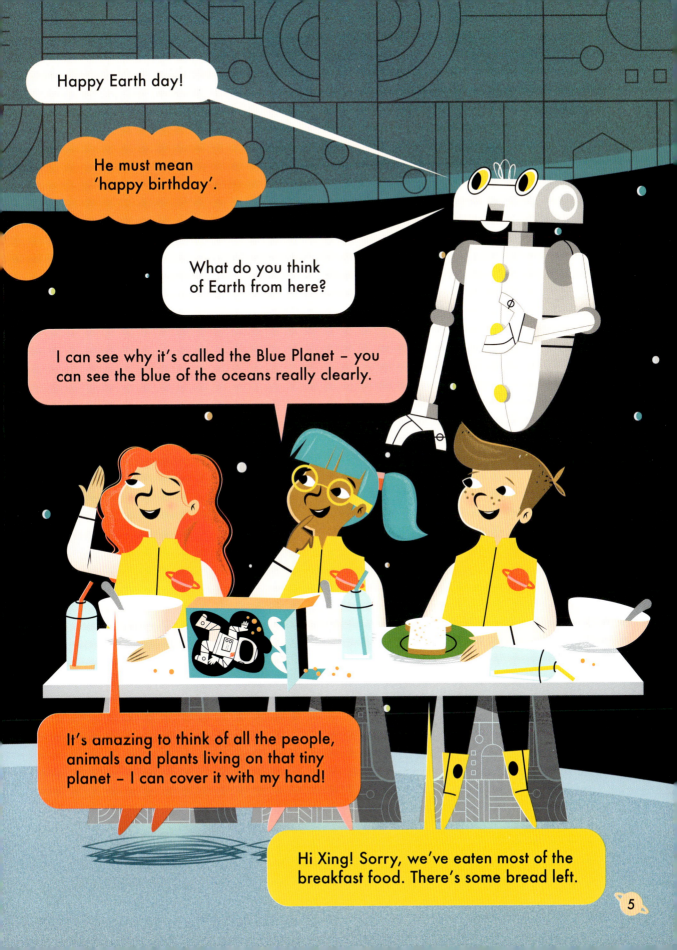

5

Pay attention, Xing!
This is how planet Earth came to be ...

Earth came into existence about 4.5 billions years ago. It formed from a swirling cloud of dust and gas orbiting the Sun.

1

Hot liquid rock, called magma, cooled to form rocky land on the surface.

The magma caused steam to form clouds. Rain from the clouds helped create the oceans, along with ice from comets that landed on Earth.

4

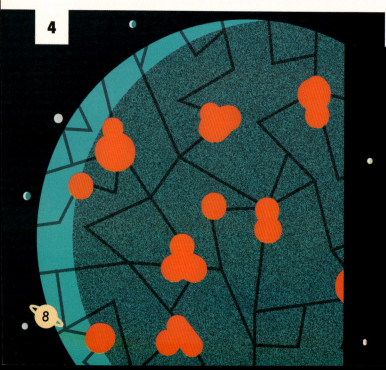

5

8

Gravity made the dust and rocks clump together until they formed one huge, hot, spinning ball.

As the young planet spun around, layers formed inside and its outside cooled to form a delicate crust.

Around 300 million years ago, Earth had one large land mass called Pangea and one ocean called Panthalassa.

The land was made from overlapping tectonic plates that split and moved to form the continents and oceans we see today.

Great, let's celebrate the birth of Earth. But what about *my* birthday?

Earth is amazing inside and out!

The inside of Earth is called the geosphere. It has four layers.

The crust is 5 to 70 km thick and made of rock and minerals. It's the bit we stand on!

The mantle is hot and made of solid rock and squishy magma.

The outer core is made from liquid iron and nickel.

The inner core is made from solid iron and nickel. Intense pressure keeps the metals solid.

It's funny to think of all those layers under your feet on Earth!

Earth orbits the Sun in 365 days, 5 hours, 59 minutes and 16 seconds. This is a year.

And we ALL have one birthday a year!

Wow! What a great view of Earth spinning and going round the Sun.

A day is 24-hours long, the time it takes Earth to spin around once.

Look at the sunlight shining on this side of the Earth!

Earth spins around an axis. For those places on Earth that are facing the Sun, it's daytime. When they spin away from the Sun, it's night-time.

What is an axis?

An axis is like an invisible stick that goes through the planet's North and South Poles. The Earth's axis is tilted at 23.5 degrees. This is why there are seasons.

The Earth rotates on its axis at the same time as it orbits the Sun. The axis always points in the same direction.

For half the year, the top of the planet, the Northern Hemisphere, is angled towards the Sun and has longer, hotter days. Meanwhile, the bottom of the planet, the Southern Hemisphere, has shorter, colder days.

23.5°

Let's take a fly-by and see for ourselves. When it's summer in Sydney in Australia, in the Southern Hemisphere ...

it's winter in New York, USA, in the Northern Hemisphere. Let's make our first stop on Earth and learn some more.

First stop: the Amazon Rainforest.

This is the perfect place to see how different Earth is from the other planets in the solar system. What do *you* think are the big differences?

Earth is a living planet, supporting billions of plants and animals!

It has oxygen we can breathe and water to drink.

The rainforest is home to half of Earth's animals and plants.

Plants absorb carbon dioxide and release oxygen into the atmosphere.

Why is Earth the only planet with life, Dr Bott?

It's all to do with Earth's position in the solar system.

It's in just the right place to be not too hot and not too cold. It's just right for life to exist. This position is called the Goldilocks or habitable zone.

Our neighbour, Venus, is too hot and Mars is too cold.

Too hot

Just right

Too cold

Back to the pod! Lots more to see and do!

This *is* a pretty exciting birthday trip!

Next stops: amazing natural landmarks!

Although Earth is unique, it does share many features with the other terrestrial planets and moons.

Look! A volcano!

Yes, Melody – this is Mauna Loa in Hawaii. It's the largest volcano on Earth. It's 4 km above sea level, and 5 km below sea level. It's tiny compared to Olympus Mons on Mars, which is 25 km high. Volcanoes have helped to shape the landscape on all the rocky planets.

And here we are on Mount Everest. This is the tallest mountain on Earth at 8.8 m high.

The tallest in the solar system is Rheasilvia on the asteroid Vesta, at 22 km high!

It's windy! I hope we don't get blown off – it's a long way to fall!

Here's Niagara Falls!
This magnificent waterfall is between Canada and the USA. The water falls 51 m down to the river below. It's not as big as the Echus Chasma waterfalls that were on Mars. Water there poured over a 4,000-m drop.

This is the Barringer Meteor Crater in the Arizona Desert. It's one of over 170 crater sites on Earth. It was made about 50,000 years ago by an iron meteorite. Our moon has over 100,000 craters including the largest in the solar system, South Pole-Aitken basin!

Now to show you the hottest and coldest places on Earth.

Can you see the two snowy patches at the top and bottom of Earth? In the centre of these are the North and South Poles, the coldest places on Earth.

It is hottest in the middle of the planet along an invisible line called the Equator. This area is always closest to the Sun.

North Pole

Equator

Xing, where would you like to go?
A cold Pole place or a hot Equator place?

Hmm, cold please!

South Pole

Happy birthday, Xing! And one last fact about Earth: it has the best parties, with the best guests! Everyone's family is here, even my mum!

Oh, you guys! This is the best birthday surprise!

Have a great time, mate!

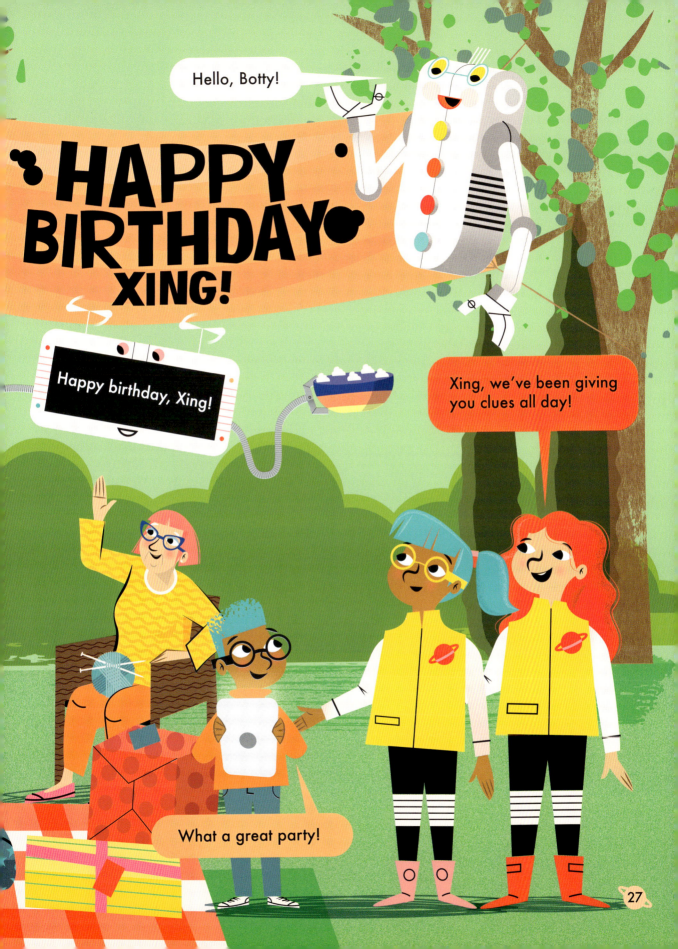

Space Academy Activities

The Space Academy gang have been so inspired by their mission to Earth, they wanted to find out more. Will you join them?

Dr Bott's Space Experiment

Earth is lit by light coming from the Sun. Light travels in a straight line, so if an object blocks the light, it casts a shadow. Let's use a shadow to make a clock!

Equipment
- A sunny day
- A stick or a pencil stuck in modelling clay
- Paper or stones
- A pen

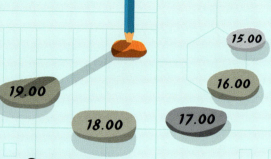

Method
Place your stick in the ground, or your pencil in the modelling clay on a piece of paper. Make sure there is space around the stick for a shadow to fall.

Draw a mark at the end of the shadow or place a stone at that point. Mark the time on the stone or the paper.

Check back each hour and record where the shadow is.

You've made a shadow clock; humans have been making these for over 5,000 years!

Outcomes
What happens to the shadow when a cloud moves over the Sun?

What happens to the shadow during the day?

Don't move your clock, then test it the next day to see if the times recorded still match up.

Another Sunlight Experiment
Write a secret message for a friend (maybe a birthday greeting) using lemon juice instead of ink. Leave the message in sunlight and watch the words magically appear!

Melody's Earth Fact

71 per cent of Earth's surface is covered with water.

Max's Extra Earth Fact

Earth spins really fast, and different places on Earth spin at different speeds. At the North and South Poles Earth is still, but at the Equator it's travelling at 460 m per second.

Xing's Earth Maths Problem

The circumference of Earth is 40,075 km. If you travelled in a straight line around the world at 24 km/h, how many days would it take you? Round your answer up to the nearest day. And for extra fun, find out how many countries the Equator passes through – what's special about this number?

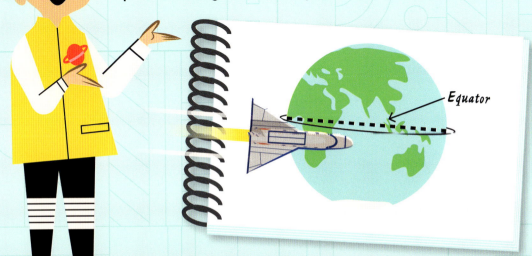

Equator

Answer: 70 days. 13 countries – it's a prime number.

Stella's Earth Picture Gallery

This is Earth. Look how much of it is covered with water, clouds and ice. Can you see any land?

The Earth and the Moon, clearly showing day and night. Where was the Sun when this was taken?

Mo's Research Project

Find out about meteorite craters on Earth. Where are they? How big are they? Then compare them to craters found on other planets.

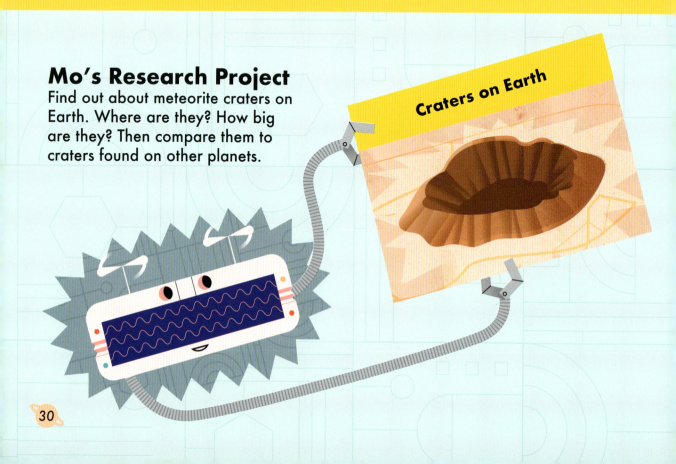

Craters on Earth

In the atmosphere above Canada, we can see the Aurora Borealis spreading across the sky. What is this? Can you see the lights on the ground below?

Look! A swirling whirling hurricane over the Pacific Ocean.

Further information

Wonderful websites

rainforest-alliance.org/resource/kids
natgeokids.com/uk/discover/science/space/facts-about-the-earth
spaceplace.nasa.gov/menu/earth
kids.britannica.com/kids/article/Earth/353074

Brilliant books

Dr Maggie's Grand Tour of the Solar System by Dr Maggie Aderin-Pocock (Buster Books, 2019)
So Many Questions About Space by Sally Spray (Wayland, 2022)
Wonders of the Night Sky by Professor Raman Prinja (Wayland, 2022)

Glossary

asteroid – a small rocky object that orbits the Sun

atmosphere – the layer of gas surrounding a planet

axis – the imaginary line around which an object, such as a planet, rotates

circumference – the measurement around the edge of a circle

comet – a lump of ice, dust and rock that orbits the Sun

core – the centre of something, such as a planet

crater – a large, bowl-shaped hole in the surface of something, such as a moon

crust – the outer or top layer of a planet

diameter – the measurement across the middle of a sphere or circle

gravity – the force of attraction that pulls one thing towards another

interstellar – describes something that is located or happens between stars

meteorite – a space rock that has fallen through a planet's atmosphere and landed on its surface

minerals – solid substances made of chemicals that form naturally on Earth, such as quartz and sulphur

moon – a natural body that orbits a planet

orbit – to travel around a star or planet

pressure – the amount of push force on something

solar system – the Sun and the objects in orbit around it

tectonic plates – massive, moving pieces of rock that make up Earth's crust

Index